Libby's Great Adventures

Pat Harvey *and* Libby

Archway Publishing books may be ordered through booksellers or by contacting:

Archway Publishing
1663 Liberty Drive
Bloomington, IN 47403
www.archwaypublishing.com
1 (888) 242-5904

ISBN: 978-1-4808-8673-5 (sc)
ISBN: 978-1-4808-8675-9 (hc)
ISBN: 978-1-4808-8674-2 (e)

Library of Congress Control Number: 2020900576

Print information available on the last page.

Archway Publishing rev. date: 02/11/2020

Acknowledgments

We are grateful for the kind support of our friends who encouraged us to write this book. We are especially thankful to Bev, Jeni, Bob, Kathy, Debbie, and Barbara, who each shared their special skills and patience.

Libby is a Cavalier King Charles spaniel who loves to travel with her best human buddy, Pat.

In *Libby's Great Adventures*, Pat helps Libby tell the story of Libby's adventures as they visit many national monuments in Washington, DC; quaint historic towns in Maryland and national parks. Along the way, Libby presents her point of view and shares interesting historical facts about each place. Even better, there are photos of Libby as she visits each site, becoming a friend to everyone she meets with her positive attitude. She offers an important lesson about the excitement of sharing adventures with a friend and provides helpful information for anyone who wants to get to know the landmarks of the nation's capital.

Inspiring and informative, this book describes the adventures of a Cavalier King Charles spaniel named Libby as she visits famous landmarks around Washington, DC and Maryland.

I love going on adventures and visiting our national treasures, whether they are the monuments in Washington, DC, quaint historic towns like Saint Michaels, Maryland, or national parks. I enjoy riding on sightseeing boats and watching the birds fly overhead.

I was born on January 31, 2012, in the sand hills of North Carolina, and at four-and-a-half months old I left to go to my forever home, where I am so happy. My life is full of love, and I am grateful every day.

Let's go exploring together, and I'll tell you about the places I've been lucky to visit and how you can have fun and learn a little something.

US Capitol
Washington, DC

    I love going on adventures. Here I am at the US Capitol building, relaxing under a shady tree, where I am watching visitors from all over the world walk around the grounds of the US Capitol on a hot day. This is where our senators and representatives meet to talk and vote on new laws that effect all of us. Sometimes they agree, and other times they argue, but their goal is to make our country a safe and happy place to live.

US Supreme Court
Washington, DC

   I am so proud to be sitting on the steps of the US Supreme Court. Nine smart judges make important decisions that interpret the meaning of the US Constitution in this building. The phrase "Equal Justice under the Law" is carved on the front of the building to remind us of the purpose of this court.

   Dedicated attorneys all over our country work hard every day to protect the rights of people. In our neighborhood courts, judges are like referees. Sometimes lawyers don't agree with the judges' decisions, and when that happens, a case can end up in the US Supreme Court. My best buddy takes me to criminal defense training with her, and I get to see lawyers who love the law.

World War II Memorial
Washington, DC

I am honored to visit this monument, and lucky to meet a nice lady who was in the US Navy during World War II. She and her daughter came to DC on a veterans' honor flight. The nice lady asked if she could take a photo of me on her lap. I gave her a great big kiss on her chin for the photo. She smiled, and it made my day.

I volunteer as a therapy dog at a nursing home, and I visited a World War II US Army veteran for over a year. I'd climb up on his lap and give him kisses. I am at this memorial in remembrance of that veteran. Take a little time to pass on the gift of love.

Korean War Memorial
Washington, DC

The monuments on the National Mall in DC give me goose bumps. There are nineteen steel soldiers, representing the army, navy, air force, and marines. They seem so real walking through a patch of bushes. I can almost feel the wind blowing their ponchos. The images on the wall opposite the soldiers show the many stories of the Korean War. Volunteers have all kinds of information they love to share with visitors. Out of respect, I don't get too close.

Reflecting Pool
Washington, DC

I am so lucky to be visiting the monuments in DC that represent this wonderful country. Here you can see the Reflecting Pool behind me, then the Washington Monument, and behind that the US Capitol.

I wish we could walk through this national park together. The experience is always an emotional one that swells my heart and reminds me of the respect we all should have for each other every day. Share a little love, and be kind to people you meet.

The White House
Washington, DC

The White House is the home of our president and his family. Sometimes presidents have a dog in their family. It seems like it would be a lot of fun to live in that big house, but I bet a president's dog really has to behave with all the visitors, staff, and expensive treasures that decorate the rooms.

Can you imagine taking a walk every day on that lawn? I wonder if a president's dog gets to smell the flowers in the Rose Garden. I would love to roam around and feel the history.

Lincoln Memorial
Washington, DC

I am excited to sit at the bottom of the steps of the Lincoln Memorial and look up at the statue of Abraham Lincoln, our sixteenth president. His strong figure sits looking over the Reflecting Pool down to the US Capitol building. During the Civil War, he signed the Emancipation Proclamation, a fancy name for the paper that helped free the slaves.

This monument is a place where many people feel safe to speak out about injustice of all kinds. I really wish I could sit on Lincoln's lap, but the nice park rangers don't let doggies go up into the building.

My Favorite Hotel
Washington, DC

Washington, DC, in August is typically really hot—I'm not kidding or exaggerating. Here I am in my favorite hotel near Farragut Square, after a two-block walk from the White House, cooling down in my comfortable room. And yes, that is a washcloth soaked in cold water draped over my head.

Smithsonian Castle
Washington, DC

Sometimes I walk along and find a surprise that tickles my tail and makes me smile. The Smithsonian Castle did that to me. It was built in 1855 and includes a visitor center where visitors can plan their trip at the Smithsonian on the National Mall. There are several museums and galleries that make up the Smithsonian on the mall in DC.

The National Air and Space Museum has moon rocks, space suits, and other exhibits from early flying machines. The National Museum of Natural History has dinosaur bones, natural gems, and even a reconstructed African elephant.

The Smithsonian Castle is a fun building to look at. When I look at it, I dream about all the things that could happen in a real castle.

Carousel at the Castle
Washington, DC

Who doesn't get excited when they see a colorful merry-go-round? This one is in front of the Smithsonian Castle. I am watching those jumping horses go up and down to music. Tourists are riding on them, and it sure looks like fun. Imagine a castle with wild horses chasing each other in a circle. It sounds funny to me, like a doggie chasing its own tail.

Farragut Park
Washington, DC

There are lots of hidden treasures in DC. Here I am checking out a beautiful garden at Farragut Park, about two blocks from the White House. It is surrounded by stores and offices. People come here for all kinds of reasons: to enjoy a little time on a park bench, to catch a bus, or to escape from a busy day. I come here to watch the people, and I enjoy rolling on the grass. What fun!

Vietnam Memorial
Washington, DC

Here are the statues of three soldiers that represent those who served in Vietnam. They are looking in the direction of the Vietnam Veterans War Memorial Wall, which is etched with names of fallen service members.

Each serviceman and servicewoman has memories to share if you just spend a little time with them.

If you get the chance to visit here, you'll see service members of all ages who are emotionally moved by the monuments. As a therapy dog, I like to comfort people, but out of respect I never get too close to these monuments.

Washington, DC

The National Mall is one of my favorite places to explore. I see all the museums and statues and visitors from around the world. I like to lap up the history. But now I'm leaving here and heading to Washington, DC's next-door neighbor, the state of Maryland.

Maryland

Follow me on my adventures to the eastern shore of Maryland. On the way I want to show you the sailing capital of the world, the town that fooled the British in the War of 1812, and the island where wild ponies roam the beaches of the Atlantic Ocean. I hope the lessons I learned during my adventures in education will stay with you for the rest of your life.

US Naval Academy
Annapolis, Maryland

There is a sightseeing boat out of City Dock in Annapolis. It travels around the US Naval Academy while the captain tells passengers about its history. It is such an interesting ride, and there are so many sailboats and other things to see. The entrance to the academy is a short walk from City Dock. Maybe next time I can walk through the grounds if they will let me.

Ego Alley—City Dock
Annapolis, Maryland

Annapolis is the capital of Maryland and the sailing capital of the world. Behind me is a narrow lane of water with a hotel. Fleet Reserve is on the right, and there are boats tied up at the marina on the left. Captains like to maneuver their boats through Ego Alley to show them off. I love going on sightseeing boats and the Cape May-Lewes Ferry, but my dream is to ride on a sailboat.

Saint Michaels, Maryland

You never know who you might run into at the Chesapeake Bay Maritime Museum by the waterfront in Saint Michaels, Maryland. This is Miss Freedom, a figurehead that used to sit on the bow of a schooner but now enjoys her days at the museum. I am sitting in a pose trying to imitate her.

Saint Michaels, Maryland

This quaint little town likes to call itself the town that fooled the British in the War of 1812. It is a place full of nice people, good food, and cute little stores. Most importantly, it is doggie friendly. It's a fun place to walk around. I love going on the sightseeing boat down the Miles River. It's a great way to learn about the local history and watch the birds fly by. The Chesapeake Bay Maritime Museum is right there along the waterfront.

Assateague Island National Seashore
Atlantic Ocean

This part of Assateague Island is a national park. Assateague is located off the coast of the eastern shores of Maryland and Virginia. The beach along the Atlantic Ocean is so peaceful when the weather is cooler and the summer sun is beating down on the sand.

I love staring out at the ocean and contemplating life as the water rolls into the beach. It's fun to walk to the edge of the water, but I must confess I don't like to get my feet wet, and I run the other way when the waves come at me.

Assateague Island—Bay Side

The bay side of the island has many little pockets of surprises. There are hiking trails, kayaking, and camping, but my favorite spot is Old Ferry Landing. I like watching visitors sitting on a park bench with a line in the water, waiting for a fish to bite, and families playing in the shallow water or trying to catch crabs. I love to roll on the ground when a friendly park ranger says hi to me.

Wild ponies walk in small herds along the beaches, narrow roads, and parking lots. The nice park rangers remind us that even though the ponies look friendly, it is not a good idea to get too close to them because they might bite or kick. I really pay attention and am quiet when they gallop past our car.

Atlantic Ocean—Alone on the Beach

I love a trip to the beach, especially the Atlantic Ocean beaches on Assateague Island. It's kind of funny since I don't like the waves chasing me. I'm not a fan of sand because it gets in my hair and makes me itchy. My best buddy brings a beach towel for me, but I still get on her lap in our beach chair. I'm so happy to be close to her.

Assateague Island—Winter

Assateague Island National Seashore is my favorite spot to be peaceful and in touch with nature. It's magical to listen to the rain or the ocean waves and let things that bother me roll out with the waves to mingle with the dolphins and other creatures, free to explore the world's seas. It might perk you up, and if you're like me, do a little dance and make a little noise. Woof, woof.

Education
A Great Adventure

Some days it's easy to learn, but sometimes I think I'll never get it. My best friend told me that education is something that no one can ever take away from you. I've been going to doggie obedience school since I was six months old, learning how to heel, come when I'm called, and do other important exercises, and it was pretty easy for me. I enter obedience shows and earn titles for completing tests.

In the past two years it has been a struggle. I just could not learn anything to do with bringing a doggie dumbbell back to my best buddy. But I kept going to classes every week, and then suddenly I could do it. And much to my surprise, it was really fun.

This week, I was in an obedience show, and it was my first time in the new category. I pulled myself together and did every exercise so well that I got a first place ribbon and a little pail full of doggie treats. Four days later, I did it again.

So whatever you are trying to learn, don't give up just because it's hard. Some days it's still hard for me and I mess up, but I don't give up. It gives you even more to love about yourself when you are proud of what you can do.

Please remember to support your friends when they are struggling. When they succeed, you do too for having supported them. Thank you to my two- and four-legged friends.

Backyard Adventure

Take your best friend for a walk, and find your next adventure.
It may be in your own backyard.

I hope that you now realize how exciting it is to share adventures with a friend. Like people, doggies come in different sizes, colors, backgrounds, or breeds. But we are all the same, doggies who want to be loved and give love.

I am a Cavalier King Charles spaniel, and my breed is known for wanting to be close to our people family and for being kind and friendly to everyone we meet.

I get to go on adventures with my best buddy, who helped put my feelings into words for *Libby's Great Adventures*. I hope that while you were reading about my travels you wagged your tail, perked up your ears, and now want to go see historic places with your family or friends. Sniff out your neighboring towns, and I'll bet you can find your own adventure.

Love,
Libby

Printed in the United States
by Baker & Taylor Publisher Services